First published in 2015
by Westmoreland Press
223 Crystal Palace Road
London SE22 9JQ

ISBN 978-0-9932660-0-3

Book design by Alex Whitworth
Cover design by Alex Whitworth

Printed and bound by Short Run Press Ltd.
Sowton Industrial Estate
Bittern Road
Exeter EX2 7LW

Distributed by Central Books
99 Wallis Road
London E9 5LN

Front cover image of Ted Hughes at Nathaniel and
Helen's wedding August 1969
Images © Dr Helen Minton

A Memoir of Ted Hughes

by Dr Nathaniel Minton

WEST
MORE
LAND
PRESS

Foreword

The idea for this short memoir was first mooted in 2007, when Bert Wyatt Brown, an American friend of Ted Hughes from Cambridge days, suggested putting together a collection of essays for a book planned to commemorate the tenth anniversary of Ted's death, in 2008.

My father, who was asked to contribute, worked on the memoir in the summer of 2007 and I helped him edit it, sending drafts over to Bert in America while my parents were on holiday in Greece. Despite our efforts, the publication was never to see the light of day as there were disagreements between the American publisher and the various authors over copyright.

My dad had always hoped to have the memoir published and since his death in November 2012 I have been hoping to publish it. Serendipitously, earlier this year I met writer and publisher, Jan Woolf, who has helped us to get the publication off the ground. I would also like to thank Martin Pickles, Alex Whitworth, Vivien Halas and Mike Swift for their help with the publication.

While this was written as a memoir of Ted Hughes, it is inevitably as much a memoir of my father himself. But while aspects of my father's own life and character come through strongly, the piece is also a testimony to his life-long friendship with Ted and his part in what he referred to as 'the gang', which was the group of Cambridge friends around Ted. It is clear that Ted was the leader of this gang as this extract from a poem by Daniel Weissbort puts it:

It began in Cambridge,
when parts, already present,
were assembled.

There was 'our Welshman';
'two jews'; an Ariel;
also an American air-or earth dweller.

As Haydn said of Handel,
'He was the master of us all',
so was Ted.

The Welshman referred to is Daniel Huws, the 'two jews' I believe to be Daniel Weissbort and my father and the American presumably Lucas Myers, another American who was a very close friend of Ted's. Ariel, I had thought was a reference to Sylvia Plath, but Daniel Huws believes it was the nickname given to David Ross.

I am taking the liberty of quoting the response to the memoir of another friend of Ted's, Richard Hollis. Richard, who very kindly cast an eye over the text and with Jan gave it another edit, said: "It reminds me so much of your father, his special earnestness and curiosity, which we loved."

We, his family, also loved these qualities about my father. We hope that he would have been pleased to see this publication, which is coming out to coincide with what would have been his 80th birthday in May 2015.

Anna Minton

London, 2015

A Memoir of Ted Hughes by Nathaniel Minton

I was nineteen when I first met Ted Hughes in Cambridge. He must have been about twenty-four. My first memory of him was in mutual friend David Ross's very large barn-like room with its high wooden ceiling, in Peterhouse College, early 1955. A huge wooden bow was resting against the wall near the door. I picked it up and tried to bend it back just a little, but failed. I felt utterly defeated; a Tom Thumb in a world of giants. The bow belonged to a giant. The giant was Ted Hughes.

Ted was a powerful, warm, charismatic figure, with a life-enhancing laugh. He enjoyed archery and was so good that he had been awarded a Cambridge half blue for it. David Ross told me that Ted, who had already left Cambridge by the time I met him, was a very good poet. At that time my university social group consisted of David and

Danny Weissbort, whom I had both known from St Paul's School in London, and Daniel Huws from Peterhouse College, who had become a friend of both David Ross and Ted. These three, David, Danny and Daniel were aspiring young poets themselves. I had a scientific background and felt lacking in knowledge of the arts and humanities. As for poetry, I knew next to nothing, except for a few lines of William Blake and Shakespeare, and a liking for Gerald Manley Hopkins.

Despite this creative vacuum, I joined what Ted always referred to as 'the gang'. I may have deluded myself into thinking that I too, one day, could become a great poet, as Ted did later. I would soar like an eagle, and, like Hölderlin reach out to the sun - but remain sane. Ted's creative gang suited me because there was always talk and discussion of poetry, which fascinated me, and I was shown scraps of verse in the making. It was like being inside a lively artistic workshop.

In retrospect I now see that joining 'the gang', which led to a friendship with Ted for the rest of his life, was in part a compensation for that first long dark year I had in Cambridge, living in lodgings on the outskirts, with a petit-bourgeois landlady who I came to know and hate as the 'rat lady'. Her parting words to me were: 'You are a Jew and I have always had gentlemen here before.' Now I know that her attitude, which frightened me, was an echo of the terrible anti-Semitism pervading Cambridge in the nineteen thirties. At around this time I also heard the fascist Sir Oswald Mosley speak at the Cambridge Union, after which I was astonished when a fellow student asked me, 'you know the Cambridge Fascist party?' I had not struggled to get into Trinity College for this. I was still immature at eighteen and had wanted a higher liberal humanities education as well as a natural science one. This was the context in which I was drawn to the friendly and deeply human Ted, who I met during my second year.

***

By early 1955, David Ross was already putting together written work to be published as a literary magazine, with the help of a generous financial gift from his father. This magazine, later to be called *St Botolph's Review,* would contain Ted Hughes' first published poetry under his own name, other promising poetry by 'the gang's' young poets and an essay on painting by the artist George Weissbort, Danny's elder brother. My own contribution was a short story based on an experience I had after a spell in hospital the previous year. During the recovery phase I met an old musician in the bed opposite me who had been at Cambridge in the nineteen thirties. I learnt later that he had died and I felt compelled to write a short story about him, which I worked on for weeks, seeking poetic prose perfection and eventually calling it *'An Impression in Hospital'.*

'The gang' was indeed a colourful group. Singing was their forte, although not mine. I would only listen while Ted sang in a strong and unforgettable way his version of the ballad of Sir Patrick Spens, resonating sonorously in the Cambridge Anchor Pub, while Luke intoned the Southern States of America's *Bo Weevil*, as if his life depended on it. Luke was Lucas Myers, a talented young American poet who came to Cambridge from Tennessee via the American Merchant Navy. With his intensity, gentleness and charming accent, he came from another world, an old culture, unknown to me. Another American friend of Luke's was Bert, a tall, friendly man with a warm smile. Luke would later become a playwright, before joining the United Nations. Luke probably came to know Ted better than any of us, with the exception of Olwyn, Ted's older sister.

During the summer term of 1955, I remember an evening curry with Ted and some others at the Taj Mahal Indian restaurant, just off Trinity Street. Ted had been working in the rose gardens, near Cambridge, and had come up for the evening. When it was time to pay, he produced a wad of brand new crisp one-pound notes. Smiling triumphantly, he savoured each note, holding, moving and counting each one, as if it was manna from heaven. As he usually had no money he felt the new notes symbolised a release from his poverty as an unknown writer. The previous year he had worked at a grammar school as a supply teacher in English and briefly as a reader at J. Arthur Rank, the film producer.

During the summer vacation of 1955 Ted stayed with me at my parents' spacious apartment in St John's Wood, which was near Regents Park and within walking distance of London Zoo. Ted was penniless at that time and needed somewhere comfortable to stay where he could write, and use as a base from which to earn a little money. We put him up on a large mattress in our front living room and he was very happy. He went out to work every morning and returned in the late afternoon. His modest job was washing up at the zoo. This gave him the opportunity to study the animals. When he got home he would sit on a chair in the hall, busy with what he called his 'scribbling'. He developed a good rapport with my father who became genuinely fond of him. My father, a distinguished eye specialist, used to show Ted some of his excellent private collection of coloured slides of the eye's retina. This was still in the pioneering days, before retinal photography had developed and become commonplace. Ted, impressed, told me he thought my father was an artist.

I think that at this time, Ted may have written his famous poem *The Jaguar*, after observing the creature closely during some of his work breaks. At some point Ted also had a job as a night watchman, although not while he was staying with me. Ted was a poor man before he became a successful and well-paid writer. He was also gentle and kind, which his later detractors have always tried to deny. I am of course referring to those who tried to demonise him after Sylvia Plath's tragic death, which I believe was due to psychiatric mismanagement.

I do not know whether I was privileged or not to have witnessed the fateful meeting of Ted and Sylvia. I did not witness their marriage a few months later, which was very private indeed.

I remember seeing an inebriated Canadian postgraduate or mature English student called Hamish, standing next to a tall girl. I could not even make out the colour of her hair in the dim light where I was standing at the St Botolph's party, held to celebrate the publication of *St Botolph's Review*. Ted suddenly appeared as if from nowhere, spotted Sylvia, for that was who the tall girl was, darted over to her and swept her away from Hamish, who had been swaying slightly, and vanished with her as quickly as he had appeared.

At another party, a few weeks later, I found myself dancing with a very attractive, bright undergraduate girl called Carla who has since disappeared from the scene. I remember Carla talking to me about the 'Ted Hughes group', 'the gang', insinuating that they all had a homosexual allegiance to each other. Nothing could be further from the truth. As for myself, I had a (mostly hidden away) muse from the West of Ireland who sometimes sang the haunting Spinning Wheel. She later left me, vanishing across the Irish Sea, leaving memories of Irish myths and culture and a love for W. B. Yeats. 'The gang', without being homophobic, had almost a contempt for the old excessively nationalistic and even sentimental poetry of Rupert Brooke and his circle. They thought they understood what real poetry was about under the leadership of Ted, who was to us at any rate, a genuine creative life force.

After the St Botolph's party I started revising for my forthcoming exams; anatomy and biochemistry, feeling a long way from the creative writing and life classes I enjoyed, and that had awakened something in me.

During my finals I felt demoralised and exhausted, and after a party on the upper floor of the student soup kitchen, crashed out and decided to give my biochemistry practical examination a miss. My practical skills were in any case seriously impaired because of the poor sight in my left eye, and complete lack of 3D stereoscopic vision.

When I did not turn up at the biochemistry practical I was deemed missing to the world. My father was contacted, who had the intuition that Ted, who he liked so much, might know where I was. How Ted was then contacted and how he found me sleeping off my hangover, I shall never know. Ted told me that I must take the practical examination, which I had missed that afternoon, in order to get my degree. I followed his instructions and owe it to him that I now have a Cambridge MA. I will be forever grateful for his kind help, as a true friend, when it was most needed.

***

In order to complete my medical studies, I had cut myself off almost completely from 'the gang' and its distractions, although I found time to try and write an occasional poem. I also sold my professional Zeiss 16 mm cine camera on which I had already shot some memorable sequences. But I was determined to become a medical doctor and ended up as a consultant psychiatrist and psychotherapist.

In 1959 I spoke to Ted on the telephone. He was then living in London with Sylvia, after their return from the USA. I was a little in awe of him after his first flush of fame with the publication of *The Hawk in the Rain,* in 1957. However, true to character he was very warm and friendly. On hearing that I was intending to take a summer vacation in Paris he insisted that on my arrival in Paris I telephone and meet his sister Olwyn.

Meeting Olwyn in Paris was a joyful experience. She was very warm, friendly and witty and appeared to be a feminine version of Ted himself. She was then working in Paris as part of the NATO Secretariat, after her English literature degree at London University. She appeared very well adjusted there, a woman of the world, with her fluent French and wide circle of friends. She introduced me to one of her girlfriends and to her very nice Hungarian Jewish boy friend – a journalist. During supper at an excellent Paris restaurant Olwyn gave me a lesson on how to speak French demonstratively, otherwise she said I would not be understood. I felt she had almost become a Parisienne herself.

I said goodbye to my new friend Olwyn, returned home, completed my medical studies and worked during my pre-registration year at a busy London postgraduate teaching hospital. It was very hard work in those days, with few days off and long weekend duties including casualty work on low pay, but it was excellent experience. I was at last a doctor, albeit overworked. My father died suddenly in the middle of that year and I was devastated. I was too confused and distressed to try to contact Ted. I did not even try to contact my oldest friend Danny, a friend of my family, who would have certainly come to the funeral had he known about it.

***

After I became fully registered with the General Medical Council I wondered what to do next in my medical career. I decided to go to Israel and work there as a doctor. Years later I understood that I was searching for my lost father in Israel, the

'Land of the Fathers'. This of course is a mystical idea, which I believe in. This type of idea, and my experience in Israel, is relevant to Ted as he too shared this interest in the mystical, and was to become interested in Israel, Jewish mysticism and later in the great poet Yehuda Amichai.

During my time in Israel, I visited Safed in the Galilee, which had been the centre of Kaballah, and the core of Jewish mysticism since the seventeenth century. Ted later became interested in the Kaballah and its influence through the Italian Renaissance, and in the development of the notion of divine love, which saturated Shakespeare's work. Towards the end of his life Ted told me that I should read his prose book Winter Pollen, which contains an essay about the connection between Shakespeare's dramatic themes and divine love, and therefore the Kaballah.

In Safed, I stayed in a small hotel where I was befriended by the owner's devoutly orthodox family. The grandfather had come out of the mists of old Jewish Poland. He had a long beard and, standing very still, silently prayed. The family told me I had to visit the Blue Room, a centuries old Kaballah synagogue. They told me exactly where I would find the caretaker, who had the key of the locked door.

The caretaker was very old and seemed to belong to a mythological tale: more spirit than man of flesh, but he was real. He opened the door of the small empty blue painted room and let me stay there on my own for a while. It was very peaceful and I felt that the Shekinah was there, the Divine Presence of God. I had felt this Presence once before as a child, whilst walking down a beautiful sunlit, West Sussex, English country lane, near our family bungalow during the Second World War. At the time the Holocaust was raging in Nazi occupied Europe and flames from millions of murdered burning innocents were rising in the sky.

Just as I came out of the blue room onto the small road outside, the heavens opened and heavy rain poured, but the old man was standing beside me and he had a large umbrella which he opened to protect me from the rain, before gently leading me back to the hotel. He must have predicted the downpour.

Safed, which I first came to know towards the end of 1961, had been the scene of bitter fighting between Israelis and Palestinian Arabs during the Israeli war of independence in 1948, which the Palestinians, both Christian and Muslim, refer to as the Catastrophe. I have later become very involved in work on conflict resolution, an area in which I feel Ted has been indirectly involved, through his founding of the international journal, *Modern Poetry in Translation*. Professor Danny Weissbort, of our old Cambridge days, edited it for forty years.

***

When I arrived back in London in the autumn
of 1962 I had the urge to make contact with Ted
again. David Ross gave me an address. It turned
out to be Sylvia's apartment in Fitzroy Road. I was
completely in the dark about Ted's recent troubles,
separation from Sylvia and the appearance of
Assia Wevill, in his life.

Ted answered the doorbell, filling the doorway
with his bulky frame. He looked grim, tired and
dishevelled, but after his surprise at seeing me,
courteously invited me in. I followed him up the
steep stairs to the open plan room on the first floor.
Sylvia was standing behind a wooden counter,
cutting either carrots or onions with complete
intensity. She seemed irritated and hardly looked
up when Ted introduced me and was obviously
more interested in preparing their meal than
entering into any conversation. I had never felt
less welcome, and wished I had not come. I gave
my apologies and took my leave. A friend, who

subsequently heard the story of this encounter, commented that Sylvia should have asked me to stay for supper, but she was not up to it and seemed to be emotionally overwhelmed.

I had not seen Sylvia since the end of my time in Cambridge, more than six years earlier, when Ted had invited me to meet her one sunny afternoon in Luke's apartment, where he had probably been staying. She had just returned from a walk in Granchester and was talking rapidly about the green meadows and the cows she had seen there, and how everything had been so beautiful. The change between then and my last glimpse of her was dramatic. Before, in Cambridge, she had been happily excited. On the last occasion she might have been on the edge of a psychotic, agitated depression. Ted took me to the door, and smiled sadly and apologetically as I said goodbye. I was never to see Sylvia again.

As yet I knew nothing about Assia who had burst into Ted's life and swept him off his feet. When I visited Ted and Sylvia uninvited, Ted may have been trying to repair their doomed relationship, no one can ever know. There is no official biography of Ted and from what I understand, there may never be one. Ted had rescued me only a few years previously during my personal crisis in Cambridge, but my crisis then was not comparable to his.

***

'Sylvia is dead, Sylvia is dead', screamed Susan Alliston, walking towards me at the corner of Lambs Conduit Street, near the Lamb Pub in Holborn, our rendezvous and a favourite meeting place for Ted's group. I was dumbfounded at the news. Sue had met both Ted and Sylvia while she was working at Faber and Faber. She was an anthropologist and was becoming a mature poet in her own right. She did not know then that she would die herself six years later from what was still untreatable Hodgkin's disease.

As I learnt more, I was able to put together what had happened. The serious press was full of it. Alvarez the English literature critic, who I have never met (but who I know has written about his own self-destructive suicidal tendencies) praised Sylvia as a genius and helped to make her famous on both sides of the Atlantic. However, I also knew it was Ted himself who found and saved Sylvia's last extraordinary poems whilst in a stupefied daze, and it was Ted himself who was responsible for getting them published. Ted was wracked with guilt and remorse. He was nearly a broken man, but the creative life force within him and his deep love for his two young children, drove him forward. Without his unstoppable creative energy he could have collapsed into a state of chronic apathy. Subsequently he told me that his own writing was his personal therapy. He became more and more his own art therapist and should be seriously studied by psychiatrists and creative psychotherapists.

Ted brought Assia to the Lamb and that is where I met her for the first time. Superficially she appeared socially poised. About a month after Sylvia's tragic demise, I started my residential psychiatric training at a hospital in the east part of Greater London. By June 1963, four months after Sylvia's death, I had passed my driving test (rather later than most) and acquired an essential car, in which I remember giving Ted and Assia a lift. Ted was sitting in the front and Assia in the back. Suddenly Assia began to shout ' I am going to kill myself, I am going to kill myself.' I was by now a young trainee psychiatrist and managed to drive slowly, keeping calm. Assia eventually calmed down herself. Ted may have told her to be quiet. I feel this incident confirms that Assia was emotionally disturbed immediately after Sylvia's death and probably remained traumatised by it for the rest of her own short life. She had already begun to identify with Sylvia and with Sylvia's suicidal behaviour, which probably drove her to eventually kill herself, together with their young daughter, six years later. Sylvia had cast her shadow from beyond the grave.

Published accounts in Assia's biography quote her work colleagues saying that Assia showed no feeling about Sylvia's death and was emotionally unmoved by it. I know this to be untrue and perhaps I should have met the biographers, who in fairness approached me, but I was not in the mood to talk to them. I believe Assia had a classical defence system of denial, which she used when writing her apparently rational suicide letter to her father. She had a very well defended persona. Life had made her hard, but I am not sure how strong.

Towards the end of 1964 and the first part of 1965 I had wanted a more central London pied-a-terre for weekends. After I had acquired one in West Hampstead for a very cheap rent I asked Ted if he wanted to make use of it during weekdays when I wasn't there. He was glad to agree and duly paid his share. I became close to Ted during this time and got to know Assia better. Ted became my mentor in literary matters, telling me to read the Epic of Gilgamesh and Max Brod's diaries and also the writings of Isaac Bashevis Singer, which he admired so much. I suppose I gave him some support, as I had more or less worked through my previous problems, which he had helped me with. He was desperately trying now to work through his bereavement after Sylvia's death and adjust himself to his new relationship with Assia. He once said to me during this time that he wanted to spend the rest of his days with her.

During the first two years, after Sylvia's death, Ted's sister Olwyn moved from her home and life in Paris to Ted's house in Devon, where he had taken his two young children. For those two years Olwyn gave them all her time, energy and tender love, becoming their mother substitute. Without a doubt she saved the situation and has never been given the full credit she deserves. I hope this memoir puts this on the record. Olwyn became an important part in the early lives of Frieda and Nicholas, Ted and Sylvia's two gifted children. They both adored Ted, who adored them.

***

I should mention that there was always a very strong psychic bond between Ted and Olwyn, obviously from their early Yorkshire childhood. Writing about this bond I am reminded about Ted's and my own interest in telepathy. While still at Cambridge I conducted a telepathy experiment with Ted and some others one evening at my parents' apartment in London. Ted and myself were the two main protagonists of the experiment, which consisted of trying to transmit a secret visual image to each other, which we would only reveal after the end of the experiment. It needed intense concentration and we had some very interesting results. In one instance, an image of a parachute in the sender was perceived in the shape of an ·umbrella by the recipient. A little prosaic, but at least the parachute did not turn into an elephant.

During the time that I had the flat in West Hampstead I have a vivid memory of sitting with Assia. We looked at each other, but did not speak. The communication was entirely non-verbal. I was struck by Assia's beauty and spirituality. Assia's gaze directed at me expressed fear, almost terror. I do not know whether she was experiencing all the terrible uncertainties of the next few years and her difficulties to come with Ted. She seemed alone, wanting help and support, which I was unable to give her, other than this non-verbal understanding of her predicament. Someone had told me she had attended some group analytical therapy sessions at the Tavistock Clinic and I thought, probably wrongly, that she had gained psychoanalytical insights into her life situation. Assia undoubtedly helped Ted to get close to Amichai's poetry, who he considered to be the Israeli genius and universal poet of the twentieth century. She also brought him close to the Kaballah.

***

I left London for Zurich in Switzerland in October 1965 to train, on a shoestring, in psychoanalysis and depth psychotherapy at the CG Jung Institute, with Jung's deputy Jolande Jacobi. Ted wished me well and reminded me to continue to read the British Medical Journal regularly. This represented his practical side and respect for scientific medicine.

My only contact with Ted whilst in Switzerland was through a dream I had of him. I was walking alongside the Lake of Zurich whilst Ted was walking next to me. His figure was large and luminous and I felt represented something of my own unfulfilled creative side, which, once again, I was trying to realise through writing a few poems; one about Abraham, another about an ancestral Jewish pedlar. I was also attempting a short story and a lyrical novel about the Second World War. Another aspect of my dream may have been connected to an intimation of Ted's own personal troubles during the period after I had last seen him in London. I subsequently learnt that he was living in Devon with Assia, his elderly parents, his two young children and Assia's child. During this period, unbeknown to me, he was obviously not coping and under enormous strain.

I got back to the UK from Zurich in May 1968, meeting my future wife at my new psychiatric job at a general medical hospital near London. I had run out of my meagre financial resources in Zurich and needed to earn my living again. My marriage was in August 1969 and Ted came to the wedding, trudging through London carrying with him his very heavy present to us of the *Shorter Oxford English Dictionary,* in which he had inscribed his good wishes for a prosperous and happy marriage. He also made a little drawing, which looked either like a face or a skull. He could draw very well. He was charming, although he also looked depressed. Assia had died earlier that year and I had been in as much darkness about this awful tragedy, as I had been about their first meeting, which started their ill-fated liaison, six or seven years earlier. Ted was full of guilt because he had not done more to try to prevent Assias' death, which may have been more inevitable than he realised. I have suggested that Sylvia had an impact on Assia's fragile psyche, before she had herself slipped through the hands of her local National Health Psychiatric Services and gassed herself. Assia, as far as I know, was not even in touch with any part of the health care system.

As the classic Greek dramatists knew, genuine tragedy was and is determined by metaphysical forces. Both Sylvia and Assia belonged to genuine tragedy. Ted himself, subsequently, became the vehicle and voice for what I believe is the greatest adaptation in English of the *Oresteia* by Aeschylus. He knew about tragedy. He was not a cruel uncaring man without feeling, but a deeply suffering and tormented man with a poignant range of feeling.

My wife and I moved to Newcastle upon Tyne at the end of 1969, where I obtained a senior assistant training position at the University Teaching Hospital Department. In October 1970 Ted came up to Newcastle to give a poetry reading. He stayed with us, together with his new wife Carol Orchard and his two young children. The children were very sweet although Nicholas started to walk round and round our sitting room, repeating several times, 'I am a ghost, I am a ghost', which I found surprising. Carol was a gracious lady and after going out for a short while after the poetry reading, returned with a gift of a silver spoon for our daughter, who was just a few months old.

During his visit to Newcastle Ted also gave me a present of his book Crow, first published in 1970, in memory of Assia and Shura. He inscribed it as follows:

To Helen–Than
Hermes, Thoth and Mercurious –
A little minus, a little plus –
In their nigredo

Were mistaken for Crow.
from Ted
Oct 16ᵗʰ 1970

We returned to London in October 1973. With Ted living in Devon, it was difficult for us to see each other, but contact continued. Ted had invited us all down to stay with him and Carol towards the end of the very hot summer of 1976, but my son was then only a few months old and my wife did not want to travel with him in the heat.

We kept in touch mainly by telephone, talking for hours at a time and I learnt more about Ted's passion for Shakespeare. We also wrote the occasional letter. In one letter (January 1985) he wrote: 'We ought really to meet you know and have a talk. Why are the desirable things so inaccessible? All it needs is a start - a track laid down, then everything follows, even tries to become a habit. So how do we make a start? We're OK I think. Frieda wrote a book. Nicholas is a postgraduate zoologist in Alaska.' In another, (April 1989) he writes: ' Danny told me about your film. How is all the therapy going? Aren't folk madder? Isn't the species fundamentally crazed? Yes of course it is. It is a baboon. A sometimes-beautiful baboon. I plug along. Plagued mainly by tiny things – distractions, of the pettiest kind. Normally they are meat and drink, but when you try to concentrate and sustain a train of thought - they act as poisons. Frieda's paintings are occasionally very beautiful – very intense and strange. Her stories are even stranger. Nicholas works in Alaska - just finished a PhD, fish biologist.'

The film he referred to was my video on *Art Therapy and Psychiatry*. Ted subsequently told me that I should ask his friend Melvyn Bragg to help me with another production. I never got round to this and when I saw Melvyn Bragg weeping in Ted and Carol's house in Devon, just before Ted's funeral service in the church nearby, I thought it was hardly the time to discuss it with him. Lord Bragg's emotional response was testimony to the deep affection Ted inspired in his close friends.

After Ted's moving funeral my imagination ran wild. I thought I heard Ted's voice, the same voice that had shouted at me down the telephone a few years earlier, some months before his colonic cancer had been diagnosed, and already too late to be treated successfully. When Ted had last spoken to me in a panic he had requested some anti-depressants, which I sent him via Olwyn. When I asked to see him before another prescription he went silent. Had I seen him and spoken to him he might have revealed a symptom of his early cancer. It is easy to be wise after the event and possibly no one could have diagnosed Ted's fatal condition any earlier and only after it was too late.

At his funeral I felt Ted had found peace in the Shekinah.

About the Author

Nathaniel Minton, known to friends and family as Than, was born in London in 1935. He went to St Paul's School and Cambridge, where he met Ted Hughes, beginning a lifelong friendship. He later studied medicine and qualified as a psychiatrist, before training in psychoanalysis and depth psychotherapy at the CG Jung Institute in Zurich. He was consultant psychiatrist at St Peter's Hospital in Chertsey for more than 20 years, where he pursued his special interests in psychotherapy and art therapy. From 2002 – 2008 he was the organiser of a series of international conferences on conflict resolution.